DEDICATION

This book is dedicated to all those who suffer from a repetitive stress
injury or cervical spine issues.

CONTENTS

Acknowledgments

ACKNOWLEDGMENTS

I would like to acknowledge Dr. Ellis and Peter Edgelow who were instrumental in my recovery.

Preface

As an individual with RSI, I tried as much as possible to list devices that someone with an RSI has actually found helpful rather than items from a catalog, having wasted money myself on things that didn't work. A lot of the suggestions are inexpensive homemade solutions or ways people with RSI's used things that aren't specifically sold as adaptive devices to adapt tasks for their disability. When my injury was really severe, some of these items made the difference between me being able to do something for myself and not being able to do it. I didn't cover adaptive devices for the computer (as there is no shortage of articles about that topic); this article is more about the rest of the activities in your daily life. Since I have Thoracic Outlet Syndrome, I sought out a lot of information for that specifically, in addition the usual suggestions for carpal tunnel, cubital1unnel, and tendonitis. A lot of the people who made suggestions also had cervical spine. Issues and certainly there is a lot of overlap in terms of what adaptations help for cervical spine issues and RSI issues.

A fellow TOS patient found web links to pictures of many of the devices as well, so you can get an idea of the commercial products. The suppliers section at the end of this document lists phone numbers for frequently cited companies so you can have catalogs sent if using a computer to look at or order products is not at all possible for you.

I listed a number of national services (mostly free) for dealing with various disability issues. You're local Center for Independent Living or other disability resource center typically has good information on local services that are useful. For example, from my local center I found out about local grocery delivery services, local transportation services for disabled people, free disability counseling of various kinds. Also each state has different special programs for disabled people and these centers will typically know what all the programs are. (In addition, these centers will also give helpful tips for navigating national programs like Social Security, Dept. of Rehab., etc.)

Disability Resource Centers:
(USA) http://www.virtualcil.net/cils/
(Canada) http://www.cailc.ca/

I took a lot of suggestions from the East Bay RSI support group and the LA RSI support group, and especially the MGH TOS forum (www.braintalk.org). (Quoted statements that don't have a specific attribution are from MGH TOS forum, as there were too many to individually cite.) My sister, Diane Diemer, who is an occupational therapist and my disability counselor who himself doesn't have use of his hands also had lots of good suggestions. The few items labeled as untested in the list mean the suggestion came from someone without an RSI, so while it probably works for an RSI, I couldn't verify it.

1) COOKING AND EATING

A few tips that I have found successful for cooking:

- Cooking vegetables before paring, trimming, and chopping them makes those tasks easier .

- Drinking with a bendable straw keeps you from having to bend your neck to drink or tip your head to get the last sip. This is especially helpful if you have TOS.

- Use the toaster oven to bake instead of the oven. The lightweight door is easier to handle. It's easy to position the toaster so that you don't have to reach very far to get a pan out of it.

- Loosely twisting and folding over open bags of food like rice to close them rather than using twist ties makes them easier to reopen.

- Use roller carts to keep near you with the items you are using to prepare dinner. Wheel it along. This is good too with heavy pans. The newer ones have two handles on them, use them both, especially when carrying water to the sink to drain.

- For vegetables and pasta I use-a sieve inside the casserole ,so I only take out the sieve and don't have to take the heavy pot.

- Adaptive devices recommended by a number of people. (Most of these are widely available at either hardware/housewares stores or from adaptive aid catalogs, but a sample supplier and picture is given for them.)

- Silicon rubber pot holders and oven mitts - These grip pots and pans belter than cloth ones so they are easier for people with reduced grip strength to use. They also insulate really well which is helpful if you don't have much sensation in your hands. I used to accidentally bum myself during the early part of my injury because I just couldn't tell I had touched something too hot.

- Very lightweight pots - I found a tiny one cup saucepan at a garage sale which is all I could lift at the beginning of my injury.

- Pots with two handles - Easier to hold if you can't lift much weight.

- Lightweight plastic bottles - I found it easier to handle milk, juice and other liquids if I transferred some to -A smaller container. The ones I got have a flip top lid that is very easy to open.

- OxoGood Grips line of kitchen utensils - This line has many types of kitchen gadgets that have big handles that are easy to hold. See pictures of many of them at http://www.chefsresource.com/oxogoodgrips.html

- When I am in extreme pain and when I cannot move my right arm, I use an self-adhesive table set. The plate does not move and that makes eating so much easier. This table set I also use in the kitchen, when I cannot hold the bowl .

- Plastic utensils are lighter and easier to handle. One woman I know with a bad RSI carries a plastic knife fork and spoon in her fanny pack for when she goes out to eat as regular cutlery is too heavy for her.

- Dazey Tabletop Automatic Electric Peeler, recommended by someone in the L.A. RSI support group.
  http://www.hometrendscatalog.com/
  Ordering information:
  8766 Automatic peeler,
  $49.95/special $44.95
  8765 Replacement blades (five), $8.50
   Home Trends
  1450 Lyell Avenue
  Rochester, NY 14606-9930
  (716) 254-6520
  (716) 458-9425

- Garlic press from "Pampered Chef" works extremely well according to the person who recommended it. You don't have to peel the garlic either. Also comes with a tool to clean out all the holes at once. You can see a picture at
  http://www.pamperedchef.com/ordering/prod_details.tpc?prodId=26463&words=garlic%20press
  (Personally, I'm a big fan of the little jars of crushed garlic from the produce section, no pressing at all ...)

- Crockpot - quite easy way to cook - just put the ingredients in and let it go. Hard to clean though unless you have someone to help you as it's heavy.

- In general, I found cookbooks labeled as quick or fast tend to have more recipes I can actually make. For example: "The PDQ (Pretty Darn Quick) Vegetarian Cookbook." by Donna Klein. This cookbook caught my eye at the book store as it promised "No chopping, peeling, slicing, coring, seeding, whipping, or blending required". On a bad day I can't use it but on a good day it's much better for cooking with TOS than most of my books; Most recipes just involve mixing together some spices and convenience food-like pre-chopped vegetables, canned goods, pre-made sauces, etc .

- Special handles that don't require much twisting for kitchen (and bathroom) taps are available.

- (untested) A couple of companies, Dynamic Living and QVC, sell battery powered handheld peelers. I'm not sure how that well that would work since you still need to do some repetitive motion.

2) CHOPPING AND MIXING

- Food processor- I had problems finding one that had a locking mechanism that wasn't painful to use and buttons that were easy to press. "Kitchen Aid" Five Cup Little Ultra Power Food Processor" and "Cuisinart Mini Prep" plus are two models that are easier to operate. I use the Mini Prep for many tasks that one would.

- Usually use a blender for since it's easier to operate and easier to clean than the usual blender. A review of the Mini Prep with a picture of it can be found at the kitchen aid site http://www.chefscatalog.com

- A small plastic stool - I use it not only to stand on, but set it on the counter and put my cutting board on top of it when I'm cooking. Otherwise the counter is too low and it flares me up.

- Cutlery with fat handles - sells an expensive set. Many house wares stores sell   cheaper ones, I got mine at IKEA.

- Curved knife - Cutting food with a rocking motion takes less force than a sawing motion. North Coast Medical and Dynamic Living sell a couple knifes like this, one for table use and one for cooking. See pictures at http://www.dynamic-living.com/rockerknives/html and http://www.dynamic-living.com/product/ulu-knife/#clear

- Electric knife sharpener - Having sharp knives considerably reduces the force needed to use them.

- VitaMinder Mixer" - This is an itty bity lightweight battery powered mixer to mix things like protein powder into milk. One source is http://shopping.yahoo.com/1389650-power-mixer-1-mixer/;_ylt=AvdBhRgvSfpHWU0KqMY2gtIGBMYu

- Stand Mixers are good if you have trouble mixing but Kitchen Aid ones that work best are very expensive. Some of the cheaper ones you have to scrape the bowl a lot during mixing which kind of defeats the purpose of a hands free

17

mixer.

3) OPENING JARS/CANS

- "Jar Pop" - A particularly easy to use jar opener for anything vacuum sealed. This company also makes a device called Can Pop for pull tab cans like cat food which I haven't tried. Available from http://www.aidsforarthritis.com/catalog/product51.html

- "Easy Opener" - A good bottle opener for water bottles or soda bottles. One company that sells it is called the "Pampered Chef ". This product can also release the seal on medium sized jars (like a salsa jar) , and has a slot so you can open a soda can as well. Has a magnet on the back so you can put it on your fridge. Available from http://www.pamperedchef.com/our_products/catalog/produ ct.jsp?productId=4992&categoryCode=KW

- A chopstick works well to pop the plastic cap off milk and juice containers

- "Bag Opener" - This is a little device with a tiny blade in it to open up food packages like frozen vegetables that are too hard for someone with an RSI to open. (You have to be able to pinch to some degree to use this.) It also has a magnet on the back. Available from North Coast Medical at http://www.ncmedical.com/item_250.html

- Krups makes a one handed can opener that leaves no sharp edges and opens any size, any shape can. Available from http://everythinghome.com

- (untested) "Open and Shut Case Kitchen Kit" - from Independent Living Products. It collects together what looks like all the openers *you* might need. "This kit comes with: the Bottle Opener/Tab Grabber that easily opens twist-off caps and pressure sealed containers; the Open Up Electric Jar Opener that can open an assortment of jars and tops, from spaghetti sauce to nail polish; Twixit Bag clips for sealing bags of potato chips and other perishable food; the Gizmo Cordless Can Opener allowing for one handed can opening operation; and the Box Topper, which opens flap-topped boxes with one hand." . You can see a picture of all the contents of the kit at http://www.activeforever.com/

4) HOUSEWORK

The big thing to remember is to let the cleaners do the work. Spray then sit and rest then wipe."

Powered Scrubbing Tools for Dishwashing and other Cleaning Tasks

- Battery operated dishwashing brushes - They now sell such brushes in the grocery store for dish soap so you don't have to scrub hard with your hands. A patient from the MGH TOS forum comments: "They work great. They're totally immiscible and run on AA batteries." Dawn Power Dish Brush is one such brand.

- Grocery stores also carry battery powered brushes for laundry strain removers and battery powered toilet brushes.

- Black & Decker Scum Buster, a battery powered scrub brush which "has loads of attachments, including an extension arm." Good for scrubbing on a variety of surfaces; tub, tile, carpets, cars, etc. Can be submersed in water. More versatile and more powerful than above small battery powered brushes.

- Vapor 2000 steam cleaner - This uses pressurized stream to clean. Apparently, you can even use it for very heavy duty tasks like cleaning ovens. "It is similar to the Shark Pro Steam Cleaner but much more beefed up. The Shark has an extremely small capacity tank and plastic scrubbers. The reheat time for action (for the Shark) is long, and the plastic scrubbers melt, read about the Vapor and was sold. They come in many sizes, I got the one about $299 on sale for $249 and free shipping. The scrubbers are metal, a variety of them and there is a floor washer too. I get enough steam to get all the heavy cleaning done in kitchen and baths. No scrubbing.

5) DISHWASHING

- Putting a dish towel or a plastic covered wire rack at the bottom of the sink when you are hand washing dishes reduces the likelihood they'll break if you accidentally drop them, as people with RSI's tend to do.

- Get some paper plates/bowls/cups and plastic silverware so you don't have to do dishes when badly flared.

- I particularly liked the Oxo Good Grips dishwashing brush and bottlebrush for hand washing dishes. They are easy to hold and dispense soap from inside the handle so you don't have to pick up a heavy bottle of dish soap. The dishwashing brush (which is named "Soap Pump Palm Brush") has a big knob like a ball for the handle. (See a picture at http://shopping.yahoo.com/786179557-oxo-good-grips-soap-pump-palm-brush/). These brushes made it possible for me to wash dishes when I could not use a sponge at all.

- Clean hand mixers and immersion blenders by running them in a bowl of soapy water.

- Norpro pot and pan scraper - The outdoors store REI sells these cheap flat tools for backpackers to scrape their cooking pots. I find that it takes less force and less repetitive motion to clean a pot that way compared to a regular scrubber sponge. (For some RSI's, this device might be difficult to hold, you would have to look at it to see if it would work for you, a picture of this device can be found at
- (http://www.norpro.com/store/products/my-favorite-colored-scraper-48-pc-dsp)

- If you've really burned something badly, try putting water and a lot of baking soda in the pan and boiling it. This will usually cause a chemical reaction that removes the black burnt part with no scrubbing at all. It can sometimes take a while, but it sure beats scrubbing.

- The spray-on foaming oven cleaners that clean without scrubbing can also be used on badly burned pans. Just make sure you get the kind designed to be used in a cold oven and, of course, rinse it off really well.

6) CLEANING FLOORS

- "I use my steam cleaner to "mop" my kitchen floor."

- "To wash the floor or sweep, the new Swiffers /Clorox Ready Mopmodels are great - no buckets of water, and light. Just remember to use your foam wrap on the handle." (You can see a picture of the Ready Mop at http://www.readymop.com/). You can use a washrag and spray ammonia on the floor in place of the expensive cloths for it.

- " I have an answer for mopping. I bought 2 big sponges - the type you use to wash the car. I spray Formula 49 (or other spray cleaners) on the floor, then step on the sponges and slide my feet around the floor - it's like ice skating. Lucking my kitchen and bathroom are small, so there is always a counter to hold onto. After I "skate" with the sponges, I use a squirting water bottle, squirt the whole floor, then skate again with paper towels under my feet. The rinsing part is important because if you leave cleaner residue on the floor it will be 5 times slipperier when it gets wet (you don't want to fall when getting out of the shower because the floor is slippery) But "rinsing" with the water squirt bottle takes the slippery-ness away."

- A suggestion from an RSI page (http://www.tifaq.com/): "To mop a floor. Wrap a towel around your mop so you have a pad of about an inch or two (to your own taste). Lightly grip the mop with straight wrists, Then dance with the mop. In other words, don't move the mop With your hands and arms, move it with your legs and feet. Wear footwear that you don't mind getting sloppy."

- Get a children's toy mop. It's lighter.

- One person in our RSI group found, in Chinatown, a broom with a cardboard handle, much lighter.

- My friend taught me this technique for cleaning up coffee or other beverage spills on carpet without having to use your hands much at all. Get a dry towel and place it over the spill. Stand on the towel right over the spill. Your weight will force the liquid into the towel, it works much better than trying to blot using the towel with your hands. You have to blot a number of times, each time moving a dry part of the towel with your feet over the spill and standing on it. After you have got the carpet pretty dry, pour a little hot water over the coffee stain and repeat the procedure with the towel. The hot water dissolves the rest of the coffee so you can blot it up, again using your feet and the towel. This technique works really well if you do it as soon as you spill the coffee, if you wait awhile it doesn't work as well.

- Vacuuming - "DONT PUSH AND PULL" Walk with it next to your leg, as you step forward, it will, when you step back it will too."

- (untested) Hoover makes a self-propelled vacuum that is not as hard to push. There is also a vacuum that vacuums, washes, and dries the floor. I'm not sure of the brand, one woman mentioned Kmart sold.

- *(Editor's Note: floormate).* There exists a robotic vacuums that vacuums by itself, I've seen it at Bed, Bath, and Beyond,

I have no idea how well it works. *(Editor's Note: Sharper Image has two - the e Vac and Roomba Discovery)*

7) DUSTING

- There are mops that look like new Swiffer's dry mop that have a microfiber pad instead for dusting that work quite well, esp. for tops of windows and walls. (My particular model is called Microfiber 2000 Mop.)

- Light weight, easier than moving a vacuum around.

- "For dust mopping I got a old fashioned dust mop and spray antistatic stuff on it. The anti-static dust cloths are also great. Use for computer screens, TV sets, general dusting, etc."

8) LAUNDRY

- "Spray and Wash laundry tablets. Easier than a liquid jug. They are good on stains also. Cheap also."

- Some laundry services have discounted rates for disabled people.

- If you have TOS, be sure to use a stool in the closet when hanging up clothes so you are not reaching overhead a lot.

- When I had people help me with laundry, I labeled sections of my closet so everything was put away in the right place and I didn't have to look through lots of hangers, which tended to flare me up.

9) CLEANING BATHROOMS

Suggestions from the MGH TOS forum:

- Note that for some bathtub/sink finishes, Ajax/Comet will gradually destroy the finish and make the tub take more and more scrubbing to clean. The Soft Scrub brand doesn't do this.

- "Baby wipes can be used for cleaning most everything in the bathroom (like that little area between the toilet seat and the tank."

- "I have found that the best thing to use product wise to clean my bathroom with the least amount of scrubbing is a mixture of borax and baking soda. 1 to 1 mix and I put orange essential oil or peppermint oil in to make it smell good. You can put it in the toilet and let it sit for 20 minutes and then you really don't need to scrub it works like magic!!! it takes off so much dirt it is unbelievable. My tiles in the tub have never looked cleaner. If you take the dry stuff and put, it into a dry tub add a little water to your cloth to make a bit of a paste then rub the paste everywhere. I can't say enough how easy it is to use."

- Rubbing alcohol on a cloth is good for removing grime from the bathtub without scrubbing.

- Several brands of bath and shower cleaners that don't require scrubbing that RSI patients have recommended: Shower

Power, Soft Scrub Brand, The Works Tub and Shower Cleaner. Generally you must leave these on for a while before rinsing off or you will need to scrub.

• " Here's my tub cleaning routine: Get some Clorox Cleanup http://www.healthyhomecare.com/solutionscleanup.html (go ahead and get a big refill too, you will use a lot and this stuff is great for toilets too) ..... and close the drain. Spray enough all over so that you have a good sized pool collecting around the drain. On your last spraying, cover all the wetted areas with Ajax w/ bleach or Soft Scrub w/ bleach ..something that will make a paste when contact with the Clorox Cleanup.

• [*Editor's comment: Be careful when mixing products as mixing bleach with ammonia can cause dangerous fumes*]: Let it soak for a few hours .... every so often rewet the upper part of the tub with what collects around the drain. Then after a few hours, go back and use a Black & Decker Scum Buster http://www.sears.com/black-decker-sbp4-scumbuster-tub-and-tile-kit/p-SPM5938433807P?prdNo=2&blockNo=2&blockType=G2 It works great for us .... I actually started doing this before the TOS set in, because I hate scrubbing the tub so bad and all the kids have finally grown and gone - no more allowance slaves   Every month I also give the comers a good spray with the mildew killers - my new favorite is: http://www.tilex.com/mildew.html. I also spray down the toilet bowl real good and with Clorox Cleanup and let it sit, often doesn't even require a brush afterwards. If you need to get under the rim, there is a gel base toilet cleaner and neat electric brush for toilets http://www.toiletwand.com .Can you tell I really hate clearing bathrooms?"

10) MAKING BEDS

- At my worst, I had trouble even pulling up blankets around me in bed, so bed making was very problematic, getting a duvet cover and a lightweight comforter really helped make it easier. I still had to get someone once a week to put anew fitted sheet on my bed and put the comforter in the newly washed duvet cover but the rest of the week I could make the bed myself by kicking the duvet in place with my feet. It wasn't exactly a neatly made bed, but it worked.

- Another person suggested getting someone to put a few safety pins around the perimeter of your sheet, blankets, and bedspread to hold everything together and make bed making easier during the week.

- In the last section – tools for comfort and/or managing flares – there are lots of comments on good pillows for RSI's as well as tips for sleeping.

11) MISCELLANEOUS HOUSEHOLD PRODUCTS

- The product "GooGone" is good for cleaning up many types of   sticky things without much scrubbing - stickers, grease, tar, tape, crayons, makeup stains. Be sure to leave it on for a while before trying to remove the stain.

- Pocket file folders - Better than regular file folders for holding receipts and other documents since the papers are less likely to fall out and need resorting.

- Hanging file crate - If I need to sort papers, I sort directly into a crate with hanging files rather than sorting papers into piles on a desk or table. This allows me to keep my arms close to my side more while sorting which is less painful for me. Keeping the box no more than half full or so also makes it easier.

- "Rolling Scissors" It's bit hard to describe these. but they are scissors that don't require any squeezing to use, you just have to lightly hold them. I could use them when I couldn't use any other scissors. Available from http://www.seniorshops.com/disabled/arthritis.cfm and North Coast Medical. I've also seen electric scissors which might work as well, but I've not tried them. Here is one source: http://www.dynamicliving.com/battery-scissors.html

- Rubber or foam grips to make it easier to hold silverware, pens. cooking utensils, and toothbrushes. Medical supply catalogs have a variety of these. Plumbers foam tubing from hardware store also works. One person I know of just got some cheap foam hair rollers from a dollar store and used the cylindrical foam part of the rollers on her pens and things.

- Screwdriver, but it was one of those inexpensive straight-line ones, and still required a less-than-ideal hand position and plenty of wrist tension to use. After searching all over, I found what I really needed at Sears with their Craftsman Model 315.111240. It's not a drill, just a light, cordless, pistol-grip reversible single-speed re-chargeable electric screwdriver with adjustable slip clutch and a LOT of torque. About $40, and worth every dime. (They sell a less expensive model as well, without the fancy clutch.) While I can't use it in some tight places, it's permitted me to continue working without jeopardizing my recovery."

12) HOUSEHOLD HEAT

- Keeping your living space warm helps with RSI recovery. You generally can get a form from your local power company for cheaper power since you have a medical problem. Your doctor must sign it. I found the

- "Vornado" space heater to be more effective in warning a room than the others that I tired.

13) LAMPS THAT ARE EASY TO TURN ON

- Using a push button is easier then twisting the typical knob on a lamp. You can get extension cords with a push button switch for all your lamps. I found at Target a floor lamp with a push button on the cord so you can just turn it on with your foot. There is also something called a "Touch Light", a flat round battery-powered light a few inches in diameter that is very easy to turn on by touch. I've seen them at Walgreen's but I'm sure many other places carry them.

- A few years ago there was a fad item called I think a Touch Lamp, that looked like a typical tabletop lamp but you turn it by just tapping the base. It worked just by touch, you didn't have to press with any force at all. Some lamp stores still carry them.

Editor's note: Make your own touch lamp:

http://www.comforthouse.com/comfort/nofumswit.html

Voice operated dimmer.

http://www.comforthouse.com/comfort/lampdimmer.html

14) PUSHING BUTTONS

- It is easier to press with your knuckle, with your wrist straight.

- Some people find it easier to use a pencil to push buttons.

15) OPENING DOORS, CABINETS, AND DRAWERS

Some general tips from the East Bay RSI Group:

- Try to arrange frequently used items to limit reaching, bending, twisting

- I stored many of the papers I needed on a frequent basis like medical reports, bills, etc in a couple open hanging file crates and an old bookshelf so they were easy to access.

- I used open baskets in my living room to organize my PT exercise equipment but keep it accessible. The more accessible it was the more I used it.

- Leave hard to open doors and cabinets unlatched.

- Use your foot to open the door the rest of the way once you have done turning the handle.

- See if you can open the drawer with your foot.

- If possible lock house door while open and pull it shut rather than locking with a key.

- Try to not overstuff drawers which can make them hard to open.

- Use a board or other object to open doors with recessed handles like some refrigerators.

- (untested) Key extensions which make keys easier to operate are available from medical supply catalogs.

- (untested) Special handles that don't require much twisting/turning/gripping for doors, oven knobs, etc. are available. Dynamic Living has one called Magic Motion that they claim you can use to open the door using just your hip. They also have a few can be installed easily over existing knobs and door handles,
  which might be helpful if you're living in apartment or are just too injured to use tools. See pictures at
  http://www.dynamic-living.com/great_grips.html and
  http://www.dynamic-living.com/door_lever.html

- Someone on the MGH TOS forum came up with a great device for opening doors in public places:

"Finding myself unable to pull open doors without triggering a painful flare up, I put together a little device using these parts: a D-shaped metal ring about an inch tall, a picture hanging hook about 10 inches of picture hanging wire. Tie the O ring to the hook using the wire. Slip the ring over your belt. (Sorry ladies won't work with a dress). To pull open a door, hook the door handle and lean back. This gets my foot in the door and from there I can use my leg and shoulder to get the door open. People look at me funny, as you can imagine. Nobody can understand why an apparently healthy looking man goes through such an absurd rigmarole. However, I much prefer funny looks to three days of constant pain."

16) CARRYING THINGS

Suggestions from various people:

- I couldn't carry a regular backpack because the straps made my TOS worse. Camping stores like REI and <u>Marmot Mountain Works</u> have lumbar packs without shoulder straps that hold almost as much as a regular daypack (basically over engineered fanny packs). For example, for a day hike, they will hold a couple liters of water, a trail book, a lunch, and some extra layers. Some of the packs come with an optional shoulder strap but as long as you don't overload the pack with really heavy things (like several textbooks), the packs are comfortable without it.

- Some people really like those rolling backpacks but I found them hard to use. Wearing wrist braces when you use them will prevent your wrists from bending or twisting if the pack goes over an uneven surface. There are lots of sources for these, here's one: http://www.bagsforme.com/bags/JS-TN88

- Roller carts for moving things around the house or unloading groceries from the car.

- Splitting your purchases into two bags of equal weight is generally easier on your hands, neck, and back   than carrying one bag asymmetrically.

- My PT really encouraged women with TOS not to use shoulder bags, just use a handbag or preferably a fanny pack.

- If you're working in a professional environment, upscale travel stores like Travel Smith have fanny packs that look more respectable and less like you just got back from a hike.

- A company called "Bagg Lady Handbags" has purses that convert from a shoulder bag to a fanny bag and look very nice, like a regular purse. They also have nice pockets to hold your checkbook, credit cards, and money like a wallet so you don't have to dig through the bag to find things which is easier 6ft your hands. They call the product "The Original Wallet Purse" and it comes in six different sizes. Bagg Lady Handbags, 13169 Twin Star Lane, Grass Valley, Ca 95949. www.bagglady.com 1-800-459-3033.

- A couple suggestions from the MGH TOS forum: "The tiniest purse I can find in order to force myself to 'travel light'" and "Slacks with POCKETS for stuff that would otherwise weigh down my purse -- cell phone, PDA. notepad, pen .. ."

- The new microfiber purses look very professional but are much lighter than the traditional leather purse. They're pretty long wearing and stain resistant as well.

17) POSITIONING/REACHING AIDES

- Kick stool - Available at office supply stores, nice to have for the kitchen if you have trouble with overhead reaching as you can easily kick the stool over to whatever cabinet you want.

- Lots of cheap lightweight stools - It is good to have a couple in every room so you don't have to move them to reach for something. It's easier on your hands. Also if you have to move the stool from room to room, you have a tendency to skip using the stool "just this once" and then after five or six times of "just this once", you find yourself flared up.

- Reacher - To help with limited mobility, a tool that allows you to grab things from a distance. All medical supply catalogs and stores have these. They vary a bit in terms of weight and how much grip strength is needed to operate them. Some have a locking mechanism so you don't have to continually grip with force while using them. An example of a reacher is given here: http://www.dynamic-living.com/reacherlock.htm

- Lightweight salad tongs - To help reach things.

- High density foam pads - I found it helpful to have some lightweight objects to help prop things to better suit my limited mobility. For example, raising my plate on the table so I didn't have to move my arms as much or raising the seat of a low chair. Two items that where particularly helpful in this regard where foam gardening knee pads (flat foam pads about 1 "x6"x18") and foam yoga blocks. Having several of each made it easy to quickly get whatever height adjustment

I temporarily needed (the foam is firm enough to maintain a constant height with weight on it). The items are lightweight so they are easy to handle (I initially used books but I couldn't lift books by myself). The specific gardening pads I use are available from Feldenkrais Resources 1-800-765-1907 for $4 a pair or ACE hardware for $2 a pair. The yoga blocks are available many places - New Age stores, yoga stores and through mail order (Gaiam). Yoga is so popular now that even my local chain bookstore and Giant Eagle (grocery store) carry these.

- "I put everything heavy at waist level. Or rather, my fiancé does. So that way, if I have to lift anything heavy, like the laundry detergent, it's easier to move."

18) PERSONAL CARE GROOMING AND BATHROOM

- Bath towels can be too heavy for a person with an RSI to lift; here are some alternatives people have figured out:

- Use one or two hand towels or washcloths.

- Use a terry cloth mitt. This has the added advantage that you don't need to grip anything.

- Backpacking stores sell a small but very absorbent towel that's very lightweight. It holds as much water as a full-size towel.

- Cloths to dry and buff your car from auto parts store are also small, lightweight, and very absorbent, so they can work well for this purpose as well.

- Turbie Twist - This is a strange little terrycloth turban to dry your hair. I found it much easier to use than a regular towel. It's also a lot lighter than a regular towel. You can get these at Longs, Walgreen's, etc.

Other ideas for the bathroom from various people:

- Electric toothbrush - The "Sonic are" tooth brush has a big fat handle and is the best one in terms of cleaning effectiveness. Best online source is www.breathcure.com

- One person's occupational therapist made a long handle for her toothbrush, about seven or eight inches long, so she didn't have to bend her arm when brushing her teeth.

- Another toothbrush suggestion - "Take your toothbrush and bring it to your favorite home improvement store. In the plumbing supplies there are a lot of different sizes of vinyl tubing. The one I have found works best is 3/8" (maybe its 1/2") mesh webbing fused into the body of the tubing. Fit it onto the handle of the toothbrush and have the store people cut the length that you need .... cost $0.13" .

- Extending bathroom mirror - You mount this device on the wall in your bathroom and then you can pull out and position the mirror close to your face. So then you don't have to bend your neck to peer into the mirror which is a really bad position if you have TOS. Some of these have a magnifying mirror.

- "Down Under Wonder Shower" - I don't have this but I've heard other TOS patients really like this. The position of the showerhead is much more adjustable than most. The showerhead is bigger with more jets so you can use it better for moist heat applications for pain control. From QVC 1-800-345-1515 (Item V15183)

- "Flicker" disposable razor - "Round and easy to hold." A bulk online source is http://www.shavesite.com/

- "Bottombudy" from Dynamic Living - For when your shoulders are too sore to reach enough to properly use toilet paper. According to the patient who recommended it, this device works better that any of the others she tried for this purpose. She also said its compact enough in its case to take with you, which apparently some of these types of products are not. She also said that the flushable wet wipes are easier to use than toilet paper. *Editor's note: "Wish I'd heard of this when my dominant hand/wrist was in a cast! Writing isn't the only thing that comes out child-like when you use the other hand. "*

- Cheap pill splitter from CVS Drug Store, which helped when I couldn't hold tiny pills well enough to break them in half.

- Putting several days' worth of vitamins and regular prescriptions into a bowl or one of those 7 day pill holders reduces how many jars you have to open every day.

- Trial size bottles of shampoo reduce the weight you have to lift.

- Leaving bottles of shampoo and other grooming products loosely closed also helps reduce the number of bottles you have to open each day.

- Long handled brush or comb - Allows you to comb your hair without raising your arms above your shoulder. The one I have from North Coast Medical has kind of a flimsy handle that bends too easily when you have tangles, so I would suggest trying a different company's product.

- Back scrubber Loofah for the shower.

- (untested) Curved bath brush from North Coast Medical - Allows you to wash your back with almost no reaching.

- (untested) "Soap Swing" from Dynamic Living- A nylon bag with a long handle that attaches to the shower wall and always keeps your soap within reach. The soft mesh bag can be used like a sponge, you don't actually have to take the soap out of the bag.

- (untested) Bracket for hairdryer allows you to mount the dryer on the wall so you don't have to hold it. Medical supply catalogs usually have these. There is also a standing model available from http://www.rkdm.com/hairmade/

  - (untested) "Armed for Anything Kit" - from Independent Living Products 1-800-377-8033. "For those with limited upper body reach and flexibility. Designed to assist people with arm/shoulder restrictions, limited reach, ... this kit contains a Long-Handled Sponge that bends and a Long-Handled Comb to extend the reach of those having difficulty reaching up and behind; a Hair Dryer Stand to eliminate the need to hold a hair dryer up above the head; a toilet Tissue Aid to assist with personal hygiene and the Aromatic Heat Therapy NeckEase and a Massager fa soothe stiff or uncomfortable muscles."

19) DRESSING

Tips from a number of different people:

- Going out in the winter was difficult because of having to put on a sweater, raincoat, gloves, and hat. I found (at Land's End) a lightweight hooded raincoat that was fleece lined and had pockets. This was much easier to deal with since I only had to put on one garment instead of five. This particular coat had Velcro closures in addition to the zippers, so I could skip the zippers when my symptoms were really bad.

- For my other outerwear with zippers, my friend tied on a couple of inches of ribbon to the zipper pulls, so they were easier to grasp.

- Get some clothing a couple sizes too big (pull on style or elastic waist, with no buttons or fasteners). Much less painful to put on.

- Wear slip-on shoes.

- For winter, I found a great, insulated pair of waterproof leather boots with Velcro closures (from a mail- order company - Maryland Square).

- You can get a long handled shoe horn from most medical supply catalogs.

- One person with TOS recommends "The most cushy insoles I can find for my shoes. They help absorb the "shock" of walking, which often transmits right through my skeleton to my collarbone.

- Nike Airs tennis shoes - "These are only tennis shoes I will buy. They have an air bubble in the heel that absorbs the shock when you walk. It makes a huge difference for me."

- "To conserve body heat (very important for RSI's) I use body oil, thermal underwear, children's "Legwarmers" to pull over my arms, and of course gloves -- a dozen gloves. fingerless, fingered, padding at the wrist, not padded, wool, cotton, leather, waterproof -- gloves for all occasions and weather conditions."

- Gloves that go all the way up past your elbows can really help with a serious RSI. One place to get such gloves is Linda Lorraine 1-415-239-2397, http://www.feri.com/llgloves/. *She will custom make the gloves and you can get a fingerless style so you can still do things while wearing them. She specifically has experience making orthopedic gloves for people with RSI's.*

- Wristies - another kind of fingerless glove to warm your wrist. These are very easy to put on and easy to pull down out of the way on your arm if you need to do something without the glove. There is one hole for your thumb and then a bigger opening, for all four fingers at once, which is why they are easier to put on, camping and sporting goods stores usually have these. A couple online sources are http://www.wristies.com/info.html (fleece ones) and http://www.thatsnifty.bizland.com/id26.html (hand knit ones).

- If you have to wear lace up shoes, there are elastic shoelaces you can just tie once and then just slip on your shoes every time you wear them. Medical supply catalogs and some sporting goods stores carry them.

- North Coast Medial and other medical supply catalogs have lots of dressing aids. I don't know anyone with an RSI who has tried these so I'm not sure how well they work.
  - There are devices to help with putting on socks.
  - There's one to help fasten buttons.
  - There's also something called a dressing stick that has hooks to help put on various garments when you have limited mobility.

- Dynamic Living has these funny Velcro button tabs to make your dress shirts look like they button but actually your shirt closes with Velcro. If you look at the picture, you'll be able to tell how to make your own homemade version (or rather have your friend make them for you since you probably can't sew if you can't button a shirt due to your RSI).

20) BRAS FOR WOMEN WITH THORACIC OUTLET SYNDROME

For women with TOS, good support can really help symptoms, but our ribs and shoulders are so sensitive that finding a comfortable one is difficult.

I read an article by someone who owned a lingerie store and she said that she found when doing fittings that many women weren't actually wearing the correct size. If you don't wear the correct size, more of the weight gets transferred to the straps, which is exactly what you don't want in TOS. So it can be helpful to go somewhere they can do a good fitting, like an old-fashioned specialty shop.

Some women with TOS find a strapless or corset type bra to work best. Ones with silicon around the top and sides of the bra to hold it up generally work better than the ones with boning, as the boning tends to dig into your ribs and really hurt. Some women's recommendations:

- "I bought one of these convertible bras from Victoria's Secret... with removable straps, that can be Qff, or normal, or racer back, or halter back, that also has the silicone beading around the elastic of the bra (top and bottom) to keep it from falling down when it is worn without straps ... Anyway, I have found that the great thing about this bra is that it works like a strapless even when I wear it with the straps, where my shoulders are not bearing the weight of my breasts, Keeping the straps on the bra keep the bra from slipping down at all like a normal strapless often does ... and even though it wears like a strapless, it doesn't feel like a strapless. So, the bra holds my chest up, and the only weight on my shoulders is from the straps that are only keeping the bra from slipping (so the straps on my shoulders support the weight of the bra only, not my breasts). It was a bit expensive (about $351 think) but it is the only bra I have worn for a year now and it is still in perfect shape and I wear it all the time:

- Natural Bra - www.naturalbra.com - A backless, strapless bra, Natural Bras are silicone "seashell" cups that stay in place by pressing onto the skin with the reusable self-adhesive. It apparently works better than it looks like it would.

Other women with TOS find a sports bra to work better. Having straps that crisscross in the back can help. Wide straps, of course, help as well. Some women's recommendations:

- sports-back bra made by Waco!..
- "Z-bra" from www.anneg.com
- "This bra works pretty good for me. It is a compression bra that I picked up at a medical supply store. They use them for people who have had breast surgery. There is not much pressure on the shoulders http://www.fstubbs.com/.

- "Elite Plus" camisole, from a Canadian company. Only bra I could wear when my TOS was severe.
  Sports bra type but with a little more shaping. It goes up to 3X.

- Decent Exposures 1-800-524-4949
  www.decentexposures.com - This is a good place to look for comfortable bras if you are a hard to fit size. They are quite willing to make custom modifications. They carry, I think, 150 sizes to begin with.

- Title 9 Sports 1-800-342-4448 -
  http://www.titleninesports.com - This company is run by
  women and they give really good information about the
  differences between models, including what cup sizes each
  model is best for. They have a rating system to show how
  supportive each model is. They have a large selection,
  underwire and not, kinds that separate the breasts and some
  more traditional sports bra types that don't. They have one
  with gel like padding in the straps.

- One woman that didn't need much support told me she
  found a camisole or tank top with a little spandex to be
  more comfortable than a bra.

21) DRIVING

If you have reduced grip strength and have a hard time holding the
wheel, here are several suggestions from different people with
RSI's:

- You can get in the gardening section of the hardware store
  (for about $3), gloves that have a crisscross pattern of sticky
  vinyl strips on the outside that makes it possible to grip the
  wheel with much less force.

- Sporting goods stores sell gloves that serve a similar
  function since weightlifters and bicyclists need gloves with
  really good gripping power. Some of these have padding in
  the palm which helps protect against the vibration from the
  steering wheel. Some even have gel filled padding which is
  especially nice.

- "Massage Grip Steering Wheel Cover", made by Auto-
  Shade. "It retails for around $20 and can be found in
  automotive stores. The Massage Grip makes the wheel quite

a bit fatter, for starters, is made of leather, which makes it easier to grip, and has strategically placed knobby plastic inset panels at three points in its circumference, on which to place your hands. Takes very little hand power on the steering wheel when you've got one of these."

- Sheepskin steering wheel cover "cost @10 and is *wonderful* for grip. No gloves needed," One online source http://steering wheel covers manufactures.alibaba.com

Other useful suggestions:

- "When driving, keep hands low on wheel (like 5 & 7). Also move up seatback so it's straight"

- Pay attention to making sure you lean all the way back in your seat. Peering over the wheel with your neck forward is just as bad for you as peering forward at the computer

- Aids for your steering wheel and parking brake to compensate for limited mobility - Available from Mobility Access, lnc - dba Mobility Systems 1-800-943-7333. www.mobilitysystems.com.

- If your shoulders are sensitive, you can get at auto parts stores a soft sheepskin padded cover for the shoulder strap. An online source is http://www.drivingcomfort.com/

- A piece of foam that is flat on one side and curved on the other placed vertically down the seat can help keep your shoulders opened up with good thoracic extension while you drive. A foam store can cut a piece to the right curvature and size for your particular needs. Another person with an RSI uses a small buckwheat filled eye pillow placed down along her spine for a similar purpose.

- "Place a pillow on lap for resting arms while driving. This makes a big difference for the arms/shoulders."
  (Editor's note: Try the "Boppie" pillow made for nursing moms that fits around your waist. Might be too big for some cars, but if it fits it's great because it provides more support tenner back and stays in place better.)

- Some winter suggestions from the LA RSI support group: "Scraping ice off your windshield using a credit card can bankrupt your wrists and fingers. Look in your local auto parts store for a long-handled, two fisted ice scrapers. Good strong handles and using two hands is so much easier on the system than one. You can even wrap the handle in pipe insulation or tennis racquet tape for a custom grip. If you can't park under cover at night, and you don't think scraping is quite your style, try carrying a single bed sheet or sheet of plastic with you. Place one end under the wipers, trap the sides in the doors, and use magnets on your trunk to hold the rear braces. In the morning, pull it off, shake off the snow and frost. Even a sheet of cardboard on the windshield will keep ice from forming on the glass.

- (untested) Seat beat strap Adjusters - Moves shoulder strap away from the base of the neck, looks useful for TOS. Available from http://www.drivingcomfort.com and from Harriet Carter. The one from driving comfort looks much better as it is safety crash tested.

- (untested) "Uni-Grip" from <u>Dynamic Living</u> - To open gas caps.

22) TRAVELING

Suggestions from a number of different people:

- Make sure you wear your wrist braces when using rolling type luggage. If you hit a bump, you will not wrench your wrist.
- Those instant hot packs and/or cold packs from the drugstore are great for travel. The kind I am talking about don't need a freezer to get cold or a microwave to get hot. They work by starting a chemical reaction so you can use them anywhere.

- Camping and travel stores have good lightweight pillows to take along. The TempurPedic travel sized pillow is particularly nice. http://www.tempurpedic.com/home/

- If Aqua therapy or hot tubs helps your pain levels, don't forget to bring your swimsuit. They have been times when I was traveling that I unexpectedly had access to a pool and was not able to use it because I hadn't thought to bring a suit.

- Think about if there's any of your PT exercise equipment or massage tools that would be helpful to bring. Obviously, some of it would be too heavy or too awkward to travel with but some of it is compact and lightweight and can help reduce pain levels when traveling. Most of the massage tools listed in this article travel well. Relaxation or meditation tapes or CDs also travel well.

- Think about if you can ship anything to where you are going instead of carrying it. If you buy things on your trip, like presents for people back home, ship rather than carry them home.

- If, like many people with RSI's, you keep your prescriptions in something easier to open than the original bottles, it's a good idea to transfer them back into those original bottles for travel. It makes it easier to get refills while traveling if you need them (and also, in the case of narcotic pain meds, to verify the pills are actually prescribed for you if airport security asks)

- "The Toll Free Hotline for disabled air travelers is available for callers from 7 a.m. to 11 p.m. Eastern Time, seven days a week. The Hotline serves two main purposes: (1) education about disabled travelers about their rights and (2) assistance in resolving real time or upcoming disability-related air travel problems. 1-800-778-4838 (voice) or 1-800-455-9880 (TTY)."

- If you have to travel internationally, traveling business class can make a big difference in how much pain you're in, esp. for those of us with disc problems. One woman I met even got a prescription from her doctor for business class for work travel which her company honored.

- (untested) 1st Class Sleeper Travel pillow - An lightweight inflatable travel pillow designed (by an airline pilot) to fit into coach airline seats and put both your lumbar and cervical spine in a neutral position and support your head. See a picture at "www.1stclasssleeper.com ". Since I haven't tried it, I don't know if it works but it looks like it could really help with the problems TOS patients have tolerating airline seats. Phone number of company is 1-866-766-6946, outside U.S.: 1-907-644-8300.

- Traveling seems to be the time you need the most help from strangers that don't know you are disabled. Most people are quite sympathetic and helpful once they understand you have a real disability. However, it can be a challenge to quickly convey an RSI disability to people in a way they understand, since of course you don't look disabled. Some solutions that people have come up with: Explaining the injury in concrete terms like "I don't have much use of my hands" or "I have a shoulder injury" can be more helpful than saying "I have an RSI", since many people don't really know what that means.

- One woman used to just say she had a. back injury even though what she really had was an RSI. The limitations are similar, for example, you need help with heavy things, and a back injury is easier to understand for most people.

- Wearing your braces or other visual reminders when traveling can be very helpful to minimize the explanations needed. For example, on the subway I can't really reach over my head to grasp the bar because of my shoulder and sometimes when its crowded people sometimes don't believe me about needing a seat. When I wear my wrist braces I got when my wrists were worse, I don't have any problems with people believing I have trouble holding a bar for a long time.

- Telling the airline or train that you are disabled when you make the reservation so it's entered into the computer can be helpful. Most of the problems I've had when traveling were from the airline or railroad staff not believing I needed what I said I needed. Somehow, having the fact that you are disabled in the computer makes the staff more likely to believe you than directly telling them. Also, you can sometimes arrange help for transferring between trains and planes if you tell them you need it when you make the reservation.

- My disability counselor described one woman who was very shy and had a hard time asking for what she needed. She got her doctor to write a short general purpose note explaining her disability, her limitations, and what she needed and she would show it to people with she had problems. These kinds of notes can also be very helpful when dealing with official staff such as that of the airlines.

23) TRANSPORTATION

- If your RSI is severe enough you can qualify for the local county's disabled transportation service, which can be very helpful, esp. for distant doctor's appointments. They will pick you up at your house and take you to your destination. If it is a shared ride system so it takes a while, but if you can't drive or take the bus for any length of time, it can really help. Be sure to fill out the form describing your limitations as they are on your worst days, not your best days.

- My local senior center said that I qualified for their transportation services since I was disabled even though I was young. They offered transportation to local grocery stores and used to offer transportation to local doctor's appointments. This probably varies widely in different communities, but it doesn't hurt to ask.

24) BOOKS ON TAPE

- Services for Books on Tape. While you can get books on tape from the library, there are some nice features about the national services for the blind and disabled. You can qualify for these services with an RSI, since RSI's affect your ability to hold a book and/or turn pages.

National Library Service for the Blind and Physically Handicapped
Library of Congress, Washington, DC 20542 www.loc.gov/nls
This free service provides popular books and many disability titles.
They have something like 90,000 titles. They even have interlibrary loan arrangements with other countries. They ship a printed or taped catalog of recent releases but you can just call and ask for specific titles. (They will take up to ten titles and ship them out a few at a time. Postage is free (including return postage). You can keep the books for five weeks. Ask for the remote control when you sign up as it's easier to push than the buttons on the tape machine they send you. Service is provided by your local state office.

Recording for the Blind
1-800-221-4792

WIW.rfbd.org

These people have textbooks and professional books. You can check them out for one year (and I think you can renew as long as you like). They will record a book for you if they don't have it, but that can take months to a year. There is an annual fee for this service (sometimes waived if you are in school or poor).

25) READING

Problems reading with an RSI tend to fall into three categories, how to get into a comfortable posture, how to keep the book open without to grip it, and how to turn pages.

For postural issues, the main idea is to try to read in a position where you're not hunched over like you probably did at the computer to get injured in the first place. An angled surface so you don't have to bend your neck helps enormously. Raising the book to eye level helps even more. For TOS patients, my PT recommends reading standing up using a music stand to get the book to eye level. There are also desks that are designed to be used standing. For reading in a sitting position, there are book stands that can be placed on a desk or table and freestanding book stands that will hold a book for you over a chair. Adjustable music stands work here as well. An adjustable height table allows you to vary your position from sitting to standing. If you need to lie flat on your back to read, there are stands which will hold the book over you. Generally, the same stands can also be adjusted to hold a book over you when you're sitting.

Most book stands have clips or elastic bands to hold the book open. There are a few small portable clips that just hold book open. You can also get a weighted bookmark sized object to hold the book open so you don't have to grip it. A low tech solution is to use a couple of thin rubber bands, one around the pages and cover on each side will keep the pages flat without you having to hold them.

If the bands are thin enough, you don't have to move them to read. Clothespins also work well to clip the book open and clip it to a slant board if you have one. Plus rubber bands and clothespins are light and portable.

To turn the pages, medical supply catalogs have various page turners available, some don't involve using your hands. A simple solution is to use the eraser end of a pencil.

Two companies that sell a variety of book stands:
Back Designs Inc. - Has lots of the products listed below.
 1-800-466-1341 or http://www.backdesigns.com/
 Levenger Tools for Reading - Has lots of products I haven't seen anywhere else.
1-800-667-8034 or www.levenger.com

Specific products recommended by various people follow:

Three small portable clips to hold books open are:

- "Bookgem" - This one is nice in that it also works as a bookstand. You can find bookstores that carry it at http://www.bookgem.com/ or write BookGem, 2857 Reposa Lane, Altadena, CA 91001-1732 USA

- "Ezbookclip" - Small compact wire clip. You can purchase it at http://www.ezbookclip.com/ or by mail order: EZ book clip, 3020 EI Cerrito Plaza No. 189, EI Cerrito, California, 94530

- "Read 'n Easy" - Designed for paperbacks. You can find bookstores that carry it at http://www.din-associates.com/. Small and Large tabbed Read-N-Easy's are $4.75 each. Orders of 3 or more $4.25 each. Shipped via standard mail. Larger orders will be sent via UPS ground or as specified.

Shipping and handling charges will be added. (Typically ordering anywhere from 1 - 4 units, shipping and handling runs approximately $2.95) Please fax or call in your order and shipping information to (248) 681-3429 or email to: info@din- associates. com

A couple stands that are designed to be placed on a desk:
- "EasyReader" - This is a nice lightweight folding bookstand, you can also use it as a clip board and as a writing tablet. You can get it at www.dynamic-living.com

- Atlas book and copyholders - This one is nice in that it also raises the book, not just holds it at an angle. You can get it at http://www.bookandcopyholders.com/ or 1-800-GET-ATLAS.

These freestanding stands are designed to be used either sitting or lying down (flat on your back with the book over you):
- "Bookvalet- www.bookvalet.com. Sold online through Back Designs Inc. http://www.backdesigns.com/ 1-800-466-1341 (Manufacturer: Worthwhile Devices, Inc., 2488 Spring Mountain Road, Saint Helena, CA 94574, 1-707-968-9978)

- "Levo" – http://www.bookholders.com/ 1-888-247-3496

These hold the book in a variety of positions:
- "LapGenie" – http://www.lapgenie.com/ - Can be used sitting on floor, on a desk, or in bed. It can raise the book quite a bit above the surface you put it on. Will hold a laptop computer. LapGenie, Ltd., PO BOX 190, Morristown, AZ. 85342, 1-623-388-0071
- (untested) "Adapt-A-Lap" -1-800-419-2354 http://www.abledata.com/abledata.cfm?pageid=113582&orgi

d=112684 - Hard to describe, see the web page.

26) WRITING

Pens (or mechanical pencils) with fat barrels like "Dr. Grip" or "Sanford's Ph.D" are pens that take the least force but some of my friends like Dr. Grip better so experiment and see what works for you. Using gel pens on glossy paper further reduces the force needed. For pencils, soft leads help reduce the force needed. There are also liquid graphite pencils that write more like a pen than a pencil and don't take much force to use. Recently, I saw an article about an innovative new pen design called PenAgain (http://www.penagain.com/) that looks like it dramatically reduces the grip strength and pressure required to write.

Several techniques to make the pen easier to grip:

- Office supply stores sell foam grips for pens.

- Foam tubing is available from medical supply catalogs or hardware stores; the latter is sold as plumbers tubing, to make the pen barrel wider.

- Sticking the pen through a whiffle ball (small hollow hard plastic ball with holes throughout the surface) www.wiffleball.com, makes it really wide if you can't grip hardly at all.

- Someone in the LA RSI support group suggests "I put a ball (a squishy one made for grasping and squishing with the fingers as a strength exercise that my PT said was a bad idea) around my pen by poking a hole through the ball and putting the pen through it. And I HAD to hold the whole apparatus softly or the ball would squish. Sometimes I just cupped my hand and rested the ball in it with the pen poking down between fingers, and wrote with the movement coming from the shoulder."

- Medical supply catalogs have devices that hold the pen for you if you can't grip at all: Some people like to use a small notepad or Palm Pilot to take notes on. The smallness of the writing surface limits how much shoulder motion is required. Sanford makes a 3 in 1 PDA stylus, pen, and mechanical pencil that have a big grip.

- I use to keep notes on my voice mail when I couldn't write at all (I had pre-programmed the number and access code on my phone so I only needed to push two buttons to access it.) You could also carry one of those small hand held recorders with you to take notes during the day. There are some that are really cheap and small if you don't need much recording time.

- For more lengthy writing tasks, a writing tablet that allows you to write on a slanted surface reduces the strain on your arms and keeps your neck in a good position. Ergonomic equipment suppliers like Back Designs and Keyboard Alternatives have a number of choices. Art supply stores sometimes have a table top easel (or drafting tables) that can serve the same function. The "EasyReader" bookstand mentioned in the above section can also be used as a writing tablet. One of my friends with an RSI just puts a 3 of 4 inch empty binder on the table (with the spine facing away from her) and writes on that, a cheap and lightweight solution.

One more suggestion from the LA RSI group. Due to my injuries, I had to change from studying Computer Science to Mathematics. However, the required amount of handwriting also gave me a lot of problems. Currently I'm using the left hand to study, and I find that using a shiny plastic cover of a cheap yellow exercise book (I rip out the paper) and a white board pen makes my writing nearly legible. Also, if I use my right hand, then writing does not require as precise a movement as a small pen, and the pen is considerably softer than even a soft lead pen. Whilst the output is not permanent, I have to do a lot less writing since I can edit my formulas in place :) Even if you do us not have RSI, this modern "slate board" allows a very nice way of doing math too! For exams I keep a stack of those covers, and the department makes a photocopy of my script.' *(Editor's comment: Keyboard Alternatives sells an add-on for Dragon Naturally speaking voice recognition software called MathTalk which handles dictation of equations and many other features of use to scientists/mathematicians)*

27) WATCHING TV/MOVIES

- Ceiling mount TV stand –"I found this at Best Buy. Sitting is my most painful position so 1 mounted the TV on the ceiling in my bedroom and I can lay down and watch it."
- Panasonic LS5 portable DVD player. - I found this really helpful for watch movies when I was flared up, I could lie in bed with my neck and back flat. It's light and easy to hold. There are lots of similar products but I liked that this one has a very high resolution screen (which is helpful when the player is so tiny) and the fact
that the screen can be moved to any angle you need

28) TELEPHONE USAGE

Adaptive Telephones

You can get free adaptive phones in California through the California Telephone Access Program 1-800- 806-1191. Other states might have similar programs. The one I have is a speaker phone with 20 spaces for preprogrammed numbers so I don't have to hold the phone or dial common numbers. I found a speakerphone works better for me than a headset, since I tended to hold my head very stiffly with the headset (my headset didn't stay on that well). The model they sent me, Panasonic KX-TS1 D8W, has good sound quality. Many of these make you sound like your speaking in a tunnel, but this one doesn't. (Place it on a hard surface as the microphone is on the underside of phone and gets muffled if you place it directly on a soft surface like a bed or sofa.)

- (untested) <u>Dynamic Living</u> has an ungodly expensive completely voice-activated phone, even has dialing by voice. I guess if you're a disabled person with more disposable income than you know what to do with, it could be a nice thing to have.

Dialing Telephones

You can just dial the operator and ask for a "manual dial" and the operator will dial the number for you. Normally there is a change for this, but if you are certified as disabled with the phone company, the fee is waived. For AT&T, I just had to call the number they have for disabled customers and tell them I had an RSI, there wasn't any doctor certification needed. AT&T's number for disabled customers is 1-800-468-8635. You can use this number for any other questions you might have, like billing questions, so you don't have to go through the normal voice mail maze to get to the person you need to speak to. As mentioned in an earlier section, it's easier to push the buttons on the phone with your knuckles, keeping your wrist straight. Some people instead find using a pencil to push the buttons easier on their hands.

LOOKING UP PHONE NUMBERS

I found phone books too heavy to lift and just turning the pages was difficult. You can use directory assistance for free, if you fill out the right form from the phone company saying you're disabled. My sister tore the Yellow Pages book into .five or six sections for me and then I could at least lift the section I needed to look at.

29) TOOLS FOR INCREASING COMFORT AND/OR MANAGING FLARES

MASSAGE TOOLS

A lot of massage tools are hard for people with RSI's to use. They are either too heavy, require too much force, or require too much grip strength. Here's some that are better for RSI patients:

- "Armaid" 1-800~549-3904 www.armaid.com - This is a device that allows you to do deep massage on your hands, forearms, and lower part of your upper arms to break up tissue adhesions and so forth. It's designed for people with repetitive stress injuries. It uses a lever to apply force, so you don't need much strength to operate it. The ball and socket hinge is stabilized by strapping it to your thigh, so you don't have to hold that part of the device. I don't think I could've used this device when my TOS was severe, but it's really helpful now. Releasing the restrictions in my forearms and elbows even makes my shoulders feel better. The company offers a 30 day money back guarantee so you can return it if it doesn't work for you.

- "TheraCane" - This is a device that allows you to massage trigger points and the like with less stress on your hands, partially because you use the device to leverage force so you don't have to press so hard, and partially because you press with the device more than your fingers. This device is esp. good for reaching points that you might not have the mobility to reach, like back and shoulders. Available from NorthCoastMedical and many other medical supply or bodywork suppliers. *Editor's Note: The one I use, because it uses your foot to apply pressure and has a variety of different massage heads, is Pressure Pointer 1-888-729-3055 http://www.mypressureproducts.com/ They will also custom make massage heads if you need a different size. The custom massage heads aren't very expensive and don't take long to make. This device also is adjustable in size for different sizes of people. There is also some information in their Pain Chart.*
The best book I found to teach you how to find and massage trigger points is "The Trigger Point Therapy Workbook" by Claire Davies. There is a lot of information on how to massage yourself in a way that minimizes stress on your hands. The book also explains what physical actions cause each trigger point so you can understand what you are doing to cause them to reappear.

- Superballs - I found lying on my back with a kid's superball under the trigger point to work better for some trigger points than the TheraCane. You can get them in many different sizes and vary them according to your needs. Sometimes starting with a small one and moving up in size works really well, especially if the trigger points are really sore. I find I use these more than the Theracane, in *fad*. I keep them in a little basket by the TV and work out the trigger points while I am watching TV.

- "Reflexology Balls" - These are somewhat flexible balls about the size of a tennis ball with little nubs all over the surface of the ball. They are nice for massaging muscles (esp. the forearm) because they are really easy to grip (even easier than the TheraCane). You can hold it with your palm and not involve your fingers much at all. You can get them at some health food stores and New Age stores.

- "Miracle balls' - sold as a kit with "The Miracle Ball Method" book by Elaine Petrone. More of a stretching method than a massage method, but it's really helpful for muscle spasms so I included it. The balls are about four inches in diameter and relatively firm, although there is some give to them. You place them under various parts to your body as shown in the book and relax over them, letting gravity do the stretch. I found they are just the right size to stretch my upper body out of the "hunched over the computer" muscle spasms. The book goes over some simple breathing techniques to do while you're doing the stretches.

- My Feldenkrais teacher showed me that if you have bad muscle spasms and use pillows and such to support your body in the position that it's trying to achieve with the spasms, it can often dramatically reduce the spasms. It's like your muscles figure out "I don't have to do this spasm to get into this position" because your body is already supported in that position with the pillows.

- (untested) TriggerWheel - I've haven't tried this but one of my PT's said some her patients really liked this. Description from Banner Therapy Products (http://www.bannertherapy.com/): "The TriggerWheel performs trigger-point therapy and myofascial release. It is especially effective at myotendon and bony junctions. Use the TriggerWheel to replace the thumb around small, difficult areas like the TMJ, occipital ridge, trapezius, parascapular, pectorals". These are also available from Stretching Online 1-800-333-1307 (http://www.stretching.com/index.php?_a=viewCat&catId=5)

Pillows of all different shapes and sizes to use while resting, reading, driving or being a passenger, during air travel, working, etc. can really help. Several people's recommendations:

- "TempurPedic" pillow - A lot of people with RSI's find these to be significantly more comfortable than a regular pillow. They come in three different heights for different neck/shoulder sizes and the fit makes a big difference in the comfort/effectiveness, so make sure you get the correct size for yourself. http://www.tempurpedic.com/home/ *Editor's Note: when shopping for memory foam, you get what you pay for really applies, but you can find brands that aren't as expensive. Thickness counts, don't settle for a thinner, cheap brand - it just isn't the same. Visco elastic, aka Memory Foam, takes some getting used to, but the effort is worth is* http://www.healthyfoundations.com/index.html

- Pillows filled with buckwheat hulls.

- One person with TOS found through a chiropractic supply company a "waterpillow". It has cushioning around a water chamber that *you* fill to the firmness you want. She commented that for her it worked better than any other neck pillow she tried, even the TempurPedic. Another person commented that she didn't like the pillow as the water got very cold in the middle of the night.

- "Soppie", a U shaped pillow that is for nursing homes. "It fits around your waist and you can rest your arms on it and ifs wonderful, and its portable."

- A small buckwheat filled *eye* pillow placed along your spine can help keep your shoulders opened out rather than hunched over. For women, *your* bra can hold this in place as you go about your day.

- "I have tried the scooped-out foam, chiro pillow. This is quite good. You must get the chiro (or whoever sells it) to measure *your* shoulder-to-neck distance, to fit the pillow correctly. It comes in 3 heights. Pillow is made of foam, scooped out in the middle, with support for the neck when you lie on your back. When you turn to the side, the foam is higher to keep your neck in alignment with the shoulder so you are not crushing anything or curving your neck. Fairly expensive, but can be a good choice."

- When you are first injured, it can be helpful to support your arms as much as possible in whatever position you are in so the strain on your neck, shoulders, and injured nerves is reduced. (It isn't a good idea to do this all the time long term, as your muscles will weaken.) Good cervical and lumbar support pillows seem to help as well. My collection of pillows included a couple different neck rolls, a couple different lumbar pillows, some inflatable pillows, a couple medium-size wedges of foam rubber, a couple of small foam rubber wedges, a big floor pillow, several standard bed pillows, a TempurPedic pillow, some rolled up hand towels, and a couple small beanbags, all of which I used at various points. Bath towels are also good for this purpose since you can roll or fold them to whatever size you need.

- In the early days of my injury, I didn't have it's the mobility to get my neck and shoulders out of the rounded hunched position I used at the computer. It would hurt to lie flat on my back but if I supported my shoulders with little wedges or pillows under them so they were in the rounded position, my shoulders would be in much less pain. (It's also probably not a good idea until do this long term, but it really helped reduce the pain until I improved *my* thoracic extension enough to be able to lie flat.)

30) BRACES FOR SLEEPING/MANAGING FLARES

While I gather it is not a good idea to immobilize a joint all the time; it can help when you are flared up, especially to sleep. Check with your doctor or PT about whether braces are a good idea for your situation, since opinions tend to vary quite a bit about the use of braces.

One TOS patient recommends:
- "The thing that helps me the most is a shoulder stabilizer. The company name on the tag is Zimmer. It's a large (12 inches wide) elasticized ace-bandage type thing with Velcro that wraps around my stomach ... and it has a small "cuff of

elasticized material attached to it that wraps around my upper arm ... it holds my arm right along my side so that I can not move my shoulder at all. It also has a second cuff that is supposed to go around the wrist (so that your lower arm is laying horizontally across your stomach) but I don't use that cuff. I like it because it allows me to relax my shoulder, and keeps my shoulder in a position that is comfortable (without having to constantly drag pillows around). It also reminds me not to use that arm when I am flaring. Since I don't use the wrist cuff, I still have use of my lower arm and hand, and I can do lots of things without causing any shoulder movement or pain." This seems it would help in retraining you to sleep with your arms down. Available from
http://www.fstubs.com/noflash/orthopedic/255.html

- My doctor gave me a new type of brace that is designed to put your hand in a sort of grooved position that maximizes the space for the carpal tunnel. You wear it when you are resting, watching TV or something, you can't do anything with the hand in the brace. But it really helps reduce the irritation at the wrist, so it helps calm down a flare even if you only wear it part of the day. My doctor recommended wearing it an hour or two on each arm once a day. The brace has a metal strip down the back of your hand to stabilize the wrist in a neutral position (attached with padded strips to the tips of three fingers and a wider strip at the wrist). Then there is a strip that you buckle around the top of your palm, pulling it hard enough to pull your palm into an arch, so your hand is in a kind of groove lengthwise. I think the strap applies enough force to slightly move the bones or something, since just putting my hand in this position without the brace didn't provide the same relief.

Some suggestions of soft braces for nighttime use:

- For stabilizing your elbow in a neutral position during the night, my PT suggests folding pillow lengthwise   around your arm and pinning it.

- "Tru-Fit" soft elbow brace.

- "Rolyan ElbowlHeel protector with Akton pad".

- One TOS paper I read suggested filling cloth tubing with batting and securing around your neck at night so your neck is supported all night long in whatever position you are in.

31) OTHER TIPS FOR SLEEPING

- A mattress "topper" or (mattress itself if you have the money) of the memory foam that the TempurPedic pillow is made of can really help you sleep if your RSI has made you more sensitive. They come in different thickness and the very thin ones don't work very well.

- Sleeping on your back with your arms down is better for TOS. A couple of long body pillows can be helpful if you tend to turn over on your stomach. One of my PI's said Target has them for $12 which is   pretty cheap for that type of pillow.

- "For me, placing the pillows around me were the only thing that allows me to sleep for any length of time. It just got THAT BAD. My PT guy had to show me how to configure the pillows and ifs the ONLY thing aside from meds that lets me get any rest are pillows under head should be staggered, pillows under arms should 'cradle' your shoulders, pillow under knees to take weight off lower back. See below: rough diagram of my pillow configuration:"

- Here is another TOS patient's description of how she sleeps: "I have managed to find a modified side/stomach sleeping position that works for me. Hopefully I'll be able to adequately describe it in words since opinions tend to vary quite a bit about the use of braces.

- One TOS patient recommends: ---"The thing that helps me the most is a shoulder stabilizer. The company name on the tag is Zimmer. It's a large (12 inches wide) elasticized ace-bandage type thing with Velcro that wraps around my stomach and it has a small "cuff" of elasticized material attached to it that wraps around *my* upper arm ... it holds my arm right along my side so that I cannot move my shoulder at all. It also has a second cuff that is supposed to go around the wrist (so that your lower arm is laying horizontally across your stomach) but I don't use that cuff. I like it because it allows me to relax my shoulder, and keeps my shoulder in a position that is comfortable (without having to constantly drag pillows around). It also reminds me not to use that arm when I am flaring. Since I don't use the wrist cuff, I still have use of my lower arm and hand, and I can do lots of things without causing any shoulder movement or pain." This seems it would help in retraining you to sleep with your arms down. Available from http://www.fstubbs.com/noflash/orthopedic/255.html

- My doctor gave me a new type of brace that is designed to put your hand in a sort of grooved position that maximizes the space for the carpal tunnel. You wear it when *you* are resting, watching TV or something, you can't do anything with the hand in the brace. But it really helps reduce the irritation at the wrist, so it helps calm down a flare even if you only wear it part of the day. My doctor recommended wearing it an hour or two on each arm once a day. The brace has a metal strip down the back of your hand to stabilize the wrist in a neutral position (attached with padded strips to the tips of three fingers and a wider strip at the wrist). Then there is a strip that you buckle around the top of your palm, pulling it hard enough to pull your palm into an arch, so your hand is in a kind of groove lengthwise. I think the strap applies enough force to slightly move the bones or something, since just putting my hand in this position without the brace didn't provide the same relief.

Some suggestions of soft braces for nighttime use:

- For stabilizing your elbow in a neutral position during the night, my PT suggests folding pillow lengthwise around your arm and pinning it.

- "Tru-Fit" soft elbow brace.

- "Rolyan ElbowlHeel protector with Akton pad".

- One TOS paper I read suggested filling cloth tubing with batting and securing around your neck at night so your neck is supported all night long in whatever position you are in.

32) OTHER TIPS FOR SLEEPING

- A mattress "topper" or (mattress itself if you have the money) of the memory foam that the TempurPedic pillow is made of can really help you sleep if your RSI has made *you* more sensitive. They come in different thickness and the very thin ones don't work very well.

- Sleeping on your back with your arms down is better for

TOS. A couple of long body pillows can be helpful if you tend to turn over on your stomach. One of my PI's said Target has them for $12 which is pretty cheap for that type of pillow.

- "For me, placing the pillows around me were the only thing that allows me to sleep for any length of time. It just got THAT BAD. My PT guy had to show me how to configure the pillows and ifs the ONLY thing aside, from meds that lets me get any rest are pillows under head should be staggered, pillows under arms should 'cradle' your shoulders, pillow under knees to take weight off lower back. See below: rough diagram of my pillow configuration:"

- Here is another TOS patient's description of how she sleeps: "I have managed to find a modified side/stomach sleeping position that works for me. Hopefully I'll be able to adequately describe it in words:

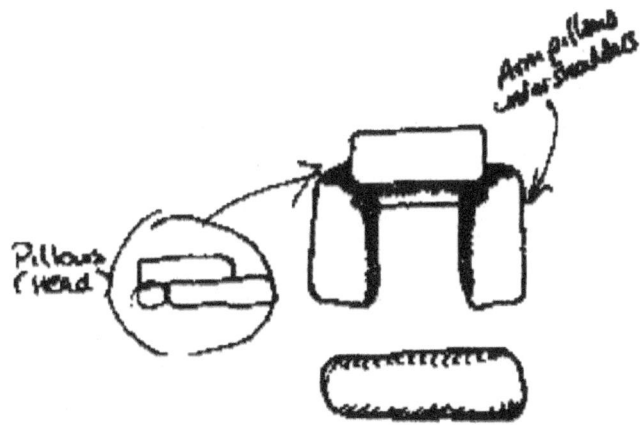

1. I use a good contour pillow - memory foam/visco elastic. I also use a memory foam/visco elastic mattress topper. This really helps

eliminate pressure points and the contour pillow supports your head/neck much better, once you get used to it.

2. I manage to lay on my side w/ same side arm straight out and not under my pillow. I make sure that the pillow supports my head and it's not on my shoulder at all- that was a huge issue for me. The head on the pillow on the shoulder progressed to producing numbness and pain within minutes - seemed to be related to the weight of the head on the shoulder ... and maybe the bad angle from a regular pillow too.

3. I make sure the other arm - the top arm is completely supported by another visco elastic pillow drawn up close to me, almost like hugging it, but arm is relaxed and on top of pillow - this pillow, while not contour, doesn't have to be memory foam but needs to be big and thick.

4. My legs are no longer hiked up at an angle .... I have a 3rd pillow that is meant for actually holding between your legs at the knees .... to take pressure off of lower back."

33) ICE PACKS

My doctor told me not to use ice for my TOS (as, while it might feel temporarily better, it overall worsens that particular condition). However, in case it's helpful for your RSI.

Here are some good homemade ice pack suggestions from the L.A. RSI support group:

- "Mix 1 part rubbing alcohol and 2 parts tap water. Freeze in a zip-lock bag. Put inside another zip-lock to guard against leakage. It gets cold but doesn't freeze hard -- just gets kind of slushy. A standard ice bag with a round screw top will be more secure than zip lock bags with the alcohol and water mixture; force all of the air out of bag to make it more moldable."

- "Saturate a half dozen or so face cloths in water & put each in a zip lock bag then freeze them. A few seconds out of the freezer & they'll conform to the shape of whatever limb you want them on-- They thaw quite quickly, but hey--you've got 5 more in the fridge & you can recycle them. I keep a couple in the fridge at work. They are great when you are traveling, too-just take the bags in your suitcase--most hotels have mini-bars with freezers and plenty of face cloths."

- Bags of frozen peas made good ice packs.

- "A simple trick for using ice packs is to hold it in place with an elastic (ACE) bandage. You can even wrap the wrist (or whatever joint) with another elastic bandage instead of using a towel around the ice pack Some people find the cooling BioFreeze spray or IcePower gel to be of help as well.

- If you use a frozen gel pack, the Thera-Med Cold Pack 1-800-327-7845 www.thera-med.com is a really good brand. The pad stays flexible when frozen and it's very durable, no squirting blue gel all over the place after a while like the usual drug store ones.

34) HEAT PACKS/HEAT TREATMENTS

I found the microwavable cloth hot packs (that have grain inside them) work better than the gel packs you get at the drug store. They get hotter and stay hot longer (about 1/2 hour).They are also easier to mold to your body. You can get them at some health food stores and New Age stores. BodySense makes a U- shaped one called NeckEase 1-877-816-3615 http://www.shopbodysense.com/painrelief.html that is especially good for getting the area around your neck/thoracic outlet warm.

Another online. commercial source is http://www.shopbodysense.com/pain-relief.html have lots of specialized shapes to fit your wrist, your neck, your low back, etc. I had a friend who sews make me some, since all they are is a bean bag with buckwheat or rice for the filling. They work better if you sew some channels or compartments so the filling doesn't shift too much. If you don't have anyone that can sew for you, one person suggested filling a tube sock with rice and tying it closed. *Editor's Note: Hard, field com (like what you feed the squirrels or deer) is also a great filling. When you microwave it, it smell nice ... almost like popcorn, and holds the heat very well. Make sure you use a durable material, as repeated headings can break down the threads, but they are a cheap alternative to commercial brands and every bit as effective.*

The following is Deborah's (a TOS patient) description of the heat treatment she gives herself when she has a severe flare. I'd done similar things when in a severe flare (the strong prescription pain killers I was given didn't seem to help at all) and it really helps. The combination of prolonged moist heat, the stretching, and drinking lots of water is somehow very effective.

"I have had a number of these 'Knock Your Socks Off and Sucker Punches out of Nowhere' pain episodes that are just absolutely, suicidal it seems at times. Nothing seems to touch the pain, your meds seemed to have forgotten why they are taken, and you feel at your absolute worse. On one hand, you just can't even imagine how it could be worse, only to wake up, to see that it is something that I have found that is beneficial to me, and a few others that I have told this to, is really an extremely easy remedy - My only 'Problem' in actually doing it and getting it done, is working up the energy and gumption to just do it- Yes, those 'dreaded pain cycles' make if unbearable to do even what you know may be best. I know that I will feel better afterwards, but I know, for me sometimes, in the throes of the devastating pain and frustration, it is sometimes impossible to see that the light at the end of the tunnel is not a freight train.

Have someone go to the drug store, or a cheap Dollar store and buy some Epsom Salts, and some cheap bath oils and bubble bath to begin with (or use your favorite if you want) ... Also, fyoUdoo;t have one already, have. someone pick up a 'Bath Pillow' for you at the same time. Use the ENTIRE Box Carton in the tub. Yes, the entire thing. Put your bath oil and bubble bath in to 'soften' the water from the salts, Run the water as hot as you can possibly stand it - This is no time to be 'weak here' - we're talking hot to the point of almost burning you. (Now, if you are having a hard time distinguishing 'hot' - have someone check it for you before you get in). But you want this water hot so that you sweat; and sweat a lot. Light some candles, put on some soft music and start to relax.

Take 4 to 6 water bottles with you or more, if you think that you can drink that much - and a stack of dry wash clothes handy to the side. And, you will be surprised at the amount of water you can drink once you start sweating. Drink up.

If you've got a shower curtain on the tub, draw that closed so that you make a 'sauna'. Close the bath door almost all the way, but not quite, esp. if your bathroom is a smaller one. This is IMPORTANT to leave the door cracked a little for ventilation so that you don't pass out from the heat. The heat from the water is going to consume the room also, and you need that as well if possible. (Again, this is dependent on room size, etc). You need to stay in that tub, with just your head exposed - water up to your neck. This is going to cover your shoulders and neck, and arms completely - Relax, take deep cleansing breathes and let it out slowly from time to time, This doesn't have to be constant the entire time you are in the tub. Within a short amount of time, you will start to sweat. Start drinking that water, with a straw if you have one so that you don't have to rise up or tilt your head and neck, as much as you can, and wiping your face to keep your face dry so that you continue sweating. And, stay in that tub for at least 2 hours, the longer you can stay put, the better. I've stayed put for up to 4 hours at a time, draining some of the water as it cools, and refilling again with hot. I'm getting pretty good with my feet at turning on the water knob!! (could be cause of the 'webbed-toes' that you get from being in the water so long! LOL) I've even managed to fall asleep in the tub in the midst of these flare-ups, (when sleep had been impossible before) waking when the water cools, and start again. Once you have started to relax and sweat, about once every half hour to 45 minutes, sit up and do some neck rolls and light arm stretches. Just gentle head/neck rolling, going completely around in a circle (no Linda Blair tricks though, that's taking it TO far). Then, go change directions and rotate in the other way. My neck and upper back will really crack and pop doing this. Sit as straight and tall as you can - feel your spine reaching and stretching' - then slowly reach your arm to the opposite leg and bend forward as slow as you can, hold for a few seconds and release going back up into a straight sitting position. Then do the other side in the same manner. (Hope this makes sense)

I also will pull on my arm, giving it a VERY GENTLE stretching. Use your own discretion on this one - I've done so after doing this process a few times to trying that particular 'stretch'. Remember to use very gentle pulling and stretching, as the water is going to have you extremely relaxed, and though it may not feel like you are applying much tension and pull, it only takes a very minimal amount since the muscles are going to be relaxed. Also, only do the arm 'pulls' if you really feel relieved of tension. When doing this one, I hold on to my wrist with one hand - with the arm to be 'pulled' directly in front of me - roll my shoulders forward and lean into the stretch, while slowly lowering my head so that my chin goes down as far as is comfortable.

I've also done torso stretches - sitting straight up again - and moving my back. Place one hand on your hip, and turn at the hip only into the hand side that you are using. If you prefer, and have the room in the tub, you can place your hand on your knee to use as the 'pull', i.e.: Left hand to right knee, right arm to your side and slightly back to balance yourself.

Once I've done all these, and the sweating and drinking all that water - it really loosens everything up - freeing up the tension in the thoracic area and relaxing the neck to allow the flare up to calm down. I make sure before I get out - that I have laid down in the water again for at least half an hour. Even if you only do these stretches a couple if times in the duration of your soak, they help."

35) RELAXATION/MEDITATION

- (CD) Letting Go of Stress by Miller and Halpem and (Tape) Healing Journey by Emmett Miller - Which relaxation tapes work for you is a pretty individual thing but these are the ones I liked best. Miller's tapes are available from 1-800-52-TAPES or www.drmiller.com . The website has suggestions of specific tapes for specific problems. "Healing Journey" is oriented to people with health problems. Some people have also mentioned liking the "Rainbow Butterfly" tape from the same people.

- (Tape Set) Breakthrough Pain: How to Relieve Pain Using Powerful Meditation Techniques by Shinzen Young (available from Sounds True 1-800-333-9185) - When you are in severe pain, it is easy to become very focused on it, which can have the effect of amplifying it. Trying to completely to ignore it on the other hand doesn't work either. This tape offers an alternative approach. You kind of distance yourself from your pain and become more of an observer, which somehow makes the pain much more bearable. You, in some sense, just sit beside your pain. I had read that meditation like this can help with pain but none of the meditation classes I took or books I read really explained how to do it. This tape is very concrete and specific and makes it easy to learn the technique. I used to listen to this tape frequently when I was in enough pain that no painkiller worked, and it really helped.

- The Yoga of Breath by Richard Rosen - This book is a very comprehensive, detailed set of exercises to improve your breathing. It can help you shift to more diaphragmatic breathing which is better for people with RSI's. There are many variations on breathing to try. There are many stretches to loosen up all parts to your body involved in breathing, including many you might not think of on your own. Most poses can be done with your arms at your side. Very few poses require any weight bearing on your arms. There are good diagrams of the exercises and the relevant anatomy. It's also very jargon free, making it accessible to people who don't practice yoga.

- (CD) Relaxation and Breathing for Meditation by Rodney

Yee (available from Gaiam 1-800-254-8464)- Has some yoga exercises similar to "The Yoga of Breath". Not as comprehensive as the book, but the selected exercises are well chosen, clearly explained, and well-paced. These exercises don't require any use of your arms.

- (CD or Book) Focusing by Eugene Gendlin - This is more of a technique than a relaxation tape, but it's a really helpful for chronic muscle tension in a way that those tapes are not. This can be a helpful book if you have a tendency to intellectualize your emotions and aren't very aware of their physical component. This
technique helps you get in touch with the physical component. By switching between the intellectual and physical components in the manner described in this book on, you can often clarify what's going on and shift it. This can have the effect of reducing the attendant muscular tension. The author developed the technique from watching hundreds of tapes of both successful and unsuccessful psychotherapy sessions and trying to extract what it was the successful patients did in their sessions. Trying the same techniques on the parts of your body that feel physical pain can sometimes be really helpful as well.

- (Tape Set) Moving Out Of Pain by Mark Reese - available from Feldenkrais resources 800-765-1907 - Again not strictly a relaxation tape, but you will generally feel very relaxed after doing these. Feldenkrais is very helpful in training you to let go of unconscious habits of chronic unnecessary muscle tension that tends to develop in response to an injury. Such muscle guarding can persist after there has been some healing of the injury and can become a problem in and of itself. This set was created for a group of chronic pain patients. (If you want an explanation of the principals of Feldenkrais, "Somatics" by Thomas Hanna is a good introduction)

- (Book) The Relaxation and Stress Reduction Workbook by Davis, Eshelman, and McKay - A very pragmatic book that give clear brief instructions on a wide variety of techniques. Tells you what each technique is for and how long each technique takes to master and get benefits from. Pain clinics often teach a number of these techniques.

- (CD) Guided Meditations: For Developing Calmness, Awareness, and Love by Bodhipaksa - I haven't had a chance to try this one but it was recommended by a TOS patient. She said it was easy to learn mediation from this CD. From the publisher - "For beginners to meditation, this CD will guide you through the most fundamental Buddhist meditation practices, and is a straightforward guide to working with your mind in order to become calmer and happier. The Mindfulness of Breathing practice will help you to develop more calmness and peace of mind; the Metta Bhavana will help you to develop a more positive attitude to yourself and others; and walking meditation is a powerful method of bringing awareness into your daily life. " More information is available at www.wildmind.org

36) SUPPLIERS

Adaptive equipment sold through medical supply catalogs and ergonomic suppliers tend to be very expensive. Some suggestions to reduce cost before I list specific suppliers used in this article:

- Often products that serves a similar function can be had for cheaper at office supply stores, hardware stores, house wares stores, and general-purpose discounters like Target. Sometimes they even have the exact same products for much less.

- Backpacking and travel outlet stores often have very lightweight household items and lightweight warm clothing.

- Dollar stores are a good place to get lightweight household items sincecheaply made stuff is often lightweight.

- Garage and rummage sales are a good place to find hand saving electric and battery-powered tools and kitchen gadgets. Plus you can generally try out the tools to see if they vibrate in an uncomfortable way or are hard to hold or use for some other reason.

- Most of this adaptive equipment is not exactly rocket science. People were able to make for me, for much cheaper, some adaptive equipment after seeing pictures in a catalog of something similar or hearing a description of it.

- Catalogs for senior citizens often have adaptable equipment similar to the medical supply catalogs for cheaper. A couple to try are Harriet Carter 1-800-377-7878 (http://www.harrietcarter.com) and Dr. Leonards 1-800-785-0880 (http://www.drleonards.com) (more medical items in this second catalog)

Medical Supply and ergonomic catalogs - Most PT's and OT's have catalogs of adaptive aids but you usually have to order through the clinic. Some catalogs you order yourself (this article draws heavily from the first three listed):

- North Coast Medical- Functional Solutions catalog 1-800-235-7054 (www.ncmedical.com)

- Dynamic Living 1-888-940-0605 (www.dynamic-living.com)

- Independent Living Products 1-800-377-8033 (http://www.activeforever.com/)

- After Therapy Catalog 1-800-634-4351

- Adaptability: Products for Independent Living 1-800-243-9232

- Enrichments 1-800-323-5547

- http://www.arthritissuppliers.com/site/371928/page53713.

- http://www.safehomeproducts.com

- www.qvc.com 1-800-367-9444 This home shopping channel obviously isn't a medical supply catalog but they do have some kitchen and cleaning equipment oriented towards people with arthritis, which also tends to work for RSI's. Battery powered kitchen gadgets and the like.

Ergonomic suppliers:

- Back Designs 1-800-466-1341 (http://www.backdesigns.com/). Has an article on cheap homemade ergonomic solutions on their web site. Lots of good chairs, pillows, reading and writing stands. They have physical therapists as consultants and it shows.

- Keyboard Alternatives and Vision Solutions 1-800-953-9262 (www.kwlt.com).This company is being renamed Solutions for Humans (www.SforH.com). Primarily adaptive computer equipment (one of the best suppliers for that) but also has reading and writing aids. They have been very helpful with detailed technical questions when I called. http://www.enablemart.com/default.aspx?store=10

37) PRODUCTS FOR COMFORT/PAIN RELIEF

- Gaiam Living Arts 1-800-254-8464 (http://www.gaiam.com/retail/gai shophome.asp) A good mail order source for things like self-massage tools and other items you might find in a New Age type store. They have several different categories of catalogs and the tools are spread throughout the different ones. They also have lots of more gentle exercise tapes (tai chi, pilates, etc.), which can sometimes have more exercises that a person with an RSI can do than the more standard home exercise tapes.

- Stretching Online 1-800-333-1307
  (http://www.stretching.com/index.php?_a=viewCat&catId
  =5) - Small, but carefully chosen set of self-massage tools.
  Has many that one of the PT clinics I went to
  recommended.

- Momentum98 1-800-533-4372
  (http://www.momentum98.com/massage.html) - Huge
  selection of self-massage tools of various kinds, although not
  a lot of overlap with the above Stretching Online site.

- Banner Therapy products http://www.bannertherapy.com/ -
  Has quite a variety of products: massage tools, all kinds of
  special pillows, lots of different hot and cold packs, rehab
  exercise equipment including aqua-therapy products, more
  traditional PT equipment like home traction units, TENs
  units.

- Relief*Mart 1-800-667-1969 (http://www.reliefmart.com/)
  Specializes in back and neck pain products. All sorts
  of products but especially strong on specialized pillows and
  braces.

ABOUT THE AUTHOR

Karen Diemer is an accomplished scientist receiving her Doctorate from University of California, Santa Cruz in Physics. She sustained her injury while working for Celera Genomics in Foster City, California. She has received instrumental help form Dr. Ellis as well as Peter Edgelow, RPT. She has proved resourceful in managing her disability and has complied this resource to assist other who may suffer from the same limitations.

www.ingramcontent.com/pod-product-compliance
Lightning Source LLC
Chambersburg PA
CBHW020351290526
45785CB00005B/2238